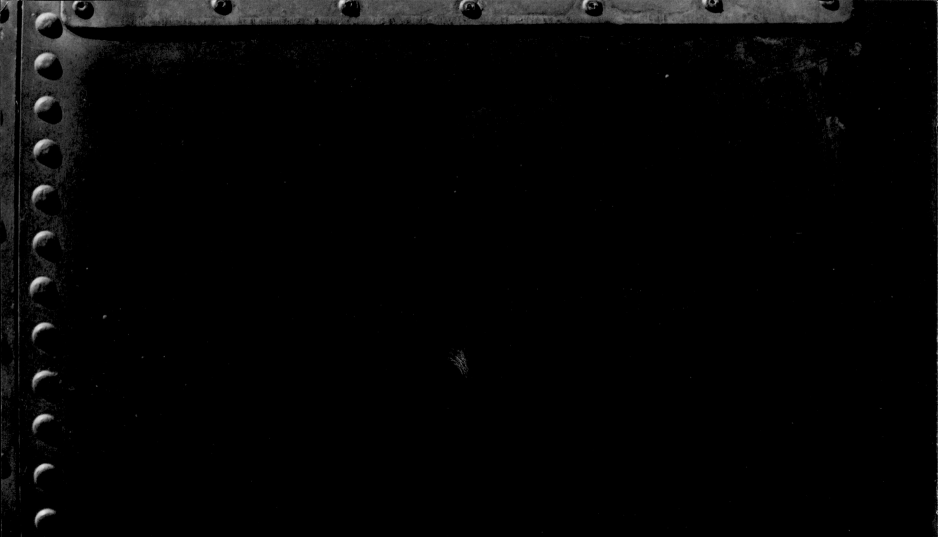

Good Question!

Why Did the Whole World Go to War?

AND OTHER QUESTIONS ABOUT. . .

World War II

STERLING CHILDREN'S BOOKS

New York

STERLING CHILDREN'S BOOKS
New York

An Imprint of Sterling Publishing
387 Park Avenue South
New York, NY 10016

STERLING CHILDREN'S BOOKS and the distinctive Sterling Children's Books logo are trademarks of Sterling Publishing Co., Inc.

Text © 2013 Martin W. Sandler
Illustrations by Robert Barrett © 2013 Sterling Publishing Co., Inc.
Maps on p.9 and p.12 by Jim McMahon © 2013 Sterling Publishing Co., Inc.
Designed by Elizabeth Phillips

Photo Credits: Corbis: 17 (top, middle) © Bettmann; Getty Images: 21, SSPL; 17 (bottom), STAFF/AFP;
The Granger Collection: 16 (top, bottom), 29; National Archives: 27; U.S. Air Force: 26

ISBN 978-1-4027-9621-0 (hardcover)
978-1-4027-9044-7 (paperback)

Library of Congress Cataloging-in-Publication Data

Sandler, Martin W.
  Why did the whole world go to war? : and other questions about World War II / by Martin W. Sandler ; illustrations by Robert Barrett.
    p. cm.
  ISBN 978-1-4027-9621-0 (hardcover) -- ISBN 978-1-4027-9044-7 (pbk.)
  1. World War, 1939-1945--Juvenile literature. I. Barrett, Robert, 1949- ill. II. Title.
  D743.7.S27 2013
  940.53--dc23
                                            2012021258

Distributed in Canada by Sterling Publishing
c/o Canadian Manda Group, 165 Dufferin Street
Toronto, Ontario, Canada M6K 3H6
Distributed in the United Kingdom by GMC Distribution Services
Castle Place, 166 High Street, Lewes, East Sussex, England BN7 1XU
Distributed in Australia by Capricorn Link (Australia) Pty. Ltd.
P.O. Box 704, Windsor, NSW 2756, Australia

For information about custom editions, special sales, and premium and corporate purchases, please contact
Sterling Special Sales at 800-805-5489 or specialsales@sterlingpublishing.com.

Manufactured in China
Lot #:
2 4 6 8 10 9 7 5 3 1
10/12

www.sterlingpublishing.com/kids

CONTENTS

Why did the whole world go to war?

The years between 1914 and 1945 were full of hardship and heroism. During that time, two world wars took place. Millions of people lost their freedom and their lives. But in the face of great difficulty, brave men and women acted with enormous courage. They fought against cruel and controlling forces.

At the start of the twentieth century, powerful European countries competed with each other for land, money, and influence. These tensions led to World War I, which lasted from 1914 to 1918. The second of these conflicts, World War II, lasted from 1939 to 1945. It involved almost every country in the world. The countries were divided into two groups. On one side were the Axis powers. They included Germany, Japan, and Italy. Germany was ruled by Adolf Hitler and his Nazi Party. Hitler wanted Germany to take over other countries and rule the world. Japan and Italy also wanted to expand and conquer other nations. Fighting against Hitler and the other Axis powers were the Allies. They included Great Britain (England, Scotland, and Wales), France, the Soviet Union, Australia, Canada, New Zealand, India, China, and the United States. They joined forces to try to stop the Axis powers from their dream of world conquest.

World War II was the deadliest war in history. More than fifteen million people lost their lives—and not all on the battlefield. More than half of those who died were ordinary people. Everyone was deeply affected by the war.

Did World War I cause World War II?

Yes. Two groups of nations fought in World War I. One side was called the Central Powers. The greatest of these nations was Germany. Its partners were Austria-Hungary, the Ottoman Empire, and Bulgaria. The other side was called the Allies. They included England, France, Russia, Japan, and Belgium.

With the help of the United States, the Allies defeated the Central Powers. The agreement that ended World War I punished Germany. Germany had to pay a large amount of money to the winning nations, give back the land it seized, and get rid of its military. Before the war, Germany had been a great nation. Now it was poor. Germany wasn't the only country left with problems. When World War I ended, many countries were still angry at each other.

How did Hitler become so powerful?

After World War I, the German people were desperate for a new leader to make Germany strong again. In the early 1930s, that leader appeared. His name was Adolf Hitler. Hitler wanted Germany to rule the world. He was the head of a German political party called the Nazi Party. In 1933, Hitler rose to the country's highest position, chancellor. Soon he did away with all the laws that gave power to the people and named himself dictator.

Hitler held dangerous, racist beliefs. He believed that white-skinned, fair-haired German people—called Aryans—were superior. He aimed to conquer or get rid of those he thought were inferior, especially Jewish people. His confidence in Germany inspired some citizens, but not all. Some thought he was a madman. But no one dared oppose him. And there was no doubt he was rebuilding Germany.

What started World War II?

By 1938, Hitler was ready to conquer other nations. In March 1938, he sent troops into Austria. That county surrendered. Then Hitler made a bold announcement. He said he was going to invade a section of Czechoslovakia. It was called the Sudetenland.

The heads of other European countries were alarmed. Hitler was bringing Europe close to another war. The leaders of England and France flew to Germany. They hoped to reason with Hitler. And they got a promise from him. He said he would not invade any other countries but only if he could take over the Sudetenland.

The leaders of England and France returned home happy. They felt sorry for the people in the Sudetenland, but they believed war had been avoided. But Hitler had lied. In March 1939, German troops took over the rest of Czechoslovakia. Then on September 1, 1939, they marched into Poland. England and France were outraged. On September 3, 1939, they declared war on Germany. World War II had begun.

The threat of war did not stop Hitler. By the end of May 1940, his armies had marched into Belgium, Denmark, Norway, the Netherlands, and Luxembourg. Huge German forces had also invaded France. On June 22, 1940, France was forced to surrender. Hitler's dream was coming true. He was about to control all of Europe.

EUROPE DURING WWII, 1941

Legend:
- Axis countries
- Axis-controlled or occupied territories
- Allied countries or territories
- Neutral countries
- ✪ Capital city
- • City

0   100 MI
0   100 KM

ICELAND — Reykjavík

NORWAY — Oslo

FINLAND — Helsinki

SWEDEN — Stockholm

DENMARK — Copenhagen

NORTH SEA

BALTIC SEA

IRELAND — Dublin

GREAT BRITAIN — London

NETHERLANDS — Amsterdam

BELGIUM — Brussels

ATLANTIC OCEAN

ENGLISH CHANNEL

Pas-de-Calais

Normandy

LUXEMBOURG

Paris

GERMANY — Berlin

Sudetenland

Prague — **CZECHOSLOVAKIA**

POLAND — Warsaw

SOVIET UNION

Moscow

Stalingrad

FRANCE

Bern — **SWITZERLAND**

LIECHTENSTEIN

Vienna — **AUSTRIA**

Budapest — **HUNGARY**

ROMANIA — Bucharest

Belgrade

YUGOSLAVIA

BULGARIA — Sofia

BLACK SEA

CASPIAN SEA

PORTUGAL — Lisbon

Madrid

ANDORRA

SPAIN

Corsica

ITALY — Rome

ADRIATIC SEA

Tirana — **ALBANIA**

Istanbul

Ankara — **TURKEY**

ASIA

Sardinia

Sicily

GREECE — Athens

MEDITERRANEAN SEA

AFRICA

MALTA

U.S.

EQUATOR

Area of map

How did Hitler take over so many countries so quickly?

Hitler and his troops took over country after country with amazing speed. Germany was successful for many reasons—it had an enormous army, and the nations it invaded were not prepared for a war. But the biggest reason was the way the German forces were fighting. It was a totally new type of warfare called *blitzkrieg*. In German, *blitzkrieg* means "lightning war." Up until now, battles were fought by slow-moving foot soldiers. The *blitzkriegs* were very different. First, hundreds of planes dropped tons of bombs onto the invaded country. Then hundreds of German tanks rolled in. They wiped out everything in their path. The tanks were followed by thousands of German soldiers. They took care of any resistance that remained. With this three-part attack plan, Hitler and Germany seemed unstoppable.

Were any countries able to resist Hitler's invasions?

By the summer of 1940, Germany controlled most of Europe. Hitler got ready to invade England. He knew it would be the most difficult invasion of all. German troops would have to be sent across the English Channel. He began by sending hundreds of German planes to bomb British factories and seaports. But pilots of the British Royal Air Force were determined to defend their country. Time after time, they beat back the German air attacks.

Hitler then changed his plan. He decided there was another way to get England to surrender. He would bomb Britain's crowded cities. His main target was London. For the next two years, German planes staged deadly bombing raids on British cities. The results were horrible. More than sixty thousand British citizens were killed.

Through it all, the British people acted with amazing courage. Millions spent long hours underground in bomb shelters. Many risked their lives battling the fires caused by the bombs. Others worked night and day to pull people out of the wreckage. The air raids did not force England to surrender. Instead, they made the brave British people more determined than ever to fight on.

THE PACIFIC DURING
WWII, 1942

SOVIET UNION

MONGOLIA

MANCHURIA

BERING
SEA

Attu

Kiska

Aleutian Islands
(U.S.)

CANADA

U.S.

SEA OF
OKHOTSK

SEA OF
JAPAN
(EAST SEA)

KOREA

JAPAN

CHINA

Nanking

Nagasaki

Tokyo

ASIA

Hiroshima

EAST
CHINA
SEA

Midway

INDIA

Hong
Kong

Okinawa

Iwo Jima

Pearl Harbor

BURMA

FORMOSA

SOUTH
CHINA
SEA

PACIFIC
OCEAN

Hawaiian Islands
(U.S.)

THAILAND

PHILIPPINE
SEA

FRENCH
INDOCHINA

PHILIPPINES

Guam

BAY OF
BENGAL

MALAYA

SINGAPORE

Borneo

EQUATOR

DUTCH EAST INDIES

NEW GUINEA

SOLOMON
ISLANDS

N

W   E

S

INDIAN
OCEAN

CORAL
SEA

AUSTRALIA

NEW ZEALAND

Axis countries

Axis-controlled
countries or
territories

Allied countries
or territories

Neutral
countries

Capital city

City

0   500 MI

0   800 KM

Area of map

U.S.

EQUATOR

★12★

Why did Japan attack its neighbors?

hen World War I ended, Japan felt cheated. It had fought on the winning side. But it had not gained any new territory. After the war, Japan came under the control of military leaders. They wanted Japan to become a world power, but they knew they had a big problem. Japan was a small island nation. It had very little coal or iron. It had no rubber or oil. These were all things that a world power had to have. Without them, important goods, especially military weapons, could not be made. Japan's leaders knew that there was only one way to get enough of these goods. They had to conquer other nations that had them.

In 1931, Japan sent an army into China. It captured the northern part of that country called Manchuria. This alarmed the United States and other countries. But Japan was determined to gain other territory. In 1937, another Japanese army invaded China. Japan took over an even larger part of that huge nation. Then, in 1940, Japanese forces invaded French Indochina. It gained control of much of that colony as well.

Up to this point, the United States had been selling oil, metal, and other materials to Japan. In 1940, the United States put an embargo on Japan. That meant that American companies were no longer allowed to sell any products to Japan. The United States hoped that this action would convince Japan to halt its attacks. It did not work, and Japan set its sights on the Dutch East Indies.

Day by day, things between the United States and Japan grew worse. Many American leaders felt that war between the two countries was bound to come. Most Japanese leaders felt that way, too. But they knew that the United States could produce more weapons than any other nation. They were not sure that they could win a long war against America. Their best chance of victory, they believed, would be to strike a quick, surprise attack.

What happened at Pearl Harbor?

Japan staged a surprise attack on December 7, 1941. Its target was the largest U.S. naval base, which was at Pearl Harbor, Hawaii. There, 185 American warships were lying peacefully at anchor. Included were eight of the nation's huge battleships. Even before the attack, Japanese officers knew exactly where American ships would be located. And they knew when it would be best to carry out the attack. They had received all this information from a Japanese spy.

At about eight o'clock in the morning on December 7, approximately 180 Japanese planes suddenly appeared over Pearl Harbor. They began dropping bombs and torpedoes on the American ships. The results of the surprise attack were devastating. Within minutes, five of the eight battleships were sunk or sinking, and the rest were severely damaged. Japanese planes also attacked Pearl Harbor's airfield. There they demolished almost two hundred American aircraft. The human loss was terrible. More than 2,340 American sailors, soldiers, and marines were killed. Some 1,180 were wounded.

It was the largest naval disaster in American history. And such a total defeat might have been avoided. About an hour before the Japanese planes arrived, two American radio operators spotted approaching planes on their radar screens. They informed Pearl Harbor headquarters, but the warning was ignored.

On December 8, 1941, the United States declared war on Japan. Japanese officials were overjoyed by the success of the attack. But one of their admirals felt differently. "I fear," he reportedly stated, "we have awoken a sleeping giant." On December 11, 1941, with their ally Japan now at war with America, Germany and Italy declared war on the United States. The United States was now involved in a war on two fronts, one with Japan—called the Pacific theater—and the other with the Axis powers—called the European theater.

The attack on Pearl Harbor

Who were the leaders of the war?

Adolf Hitler was an important figure in World War II. But other leaders also played a major role in the conflict:

WINSTON CHURCHILL (1874–1965) was the head of the Royal Navy in World War I. During World War II, he became head of the British government. Churchill was a brilliant speaker. Throughout the war, he rallied the British people. This was especially important during 1940 and 1941 when England faced daily bombing attacks from the Nazis.

FRANKLIN D. ROOSEVELT (1882–1945) was president of the United States for twelve years. He held office far longer than any other American president. Before World War II, Roosevelt led the United States out of its worst economic times during the Great Depression. During the war, he was a great leader. He died just a few months before the end of the war.

BENITO MUSSOLINI (1883–1945) was the leader of Italy during most of World War II. He named himself dictator of Italy even before Hitler became dictator of Germany. Under Mussolini, Italy became Germany's closest ally.

JOSEPH STALIN (1879–1953) was the dictator of Russia. He was responsible for turning his country into a powerful nation. But he was a terribly ruthless leader. He had millions of Russian people who opposed him either put into prison or put to death.

HIROHITO (1901–1989) was the emperor of Japan during World War II. Many Japanese people regarded him as a god. But he actually had very little power. By the time World War II began, military leaders ruled Japan.

German U-boat attack

What was the longest battle of the war?

The Battle of the Atlantic was the longest battle of the war. It lasted more than four years. To fight against the Nazis, American troops had to cross the Atlantic Ocean in ships. U.S. ships also had to cross the Atlantic to deliver supplies to England. The Germans knew how important it was to stop these ships. And they had a very special weapon. It was a deadly type of submarine called a U-boat. U-boats could hide themselves deep in the ocean. They could travel extremely fast. They fired large torpedoes that could sink ships of any size.

For more than three years, U-boats ruled the Atlantic. They sank more than two thousand American and British ships. They sent more than thirteen million tons of supplies to the bottom of the ocean. It was an alarming situation. Something had to be done about it. If not, the United States and its allies were in danger of losing the war.

Finally, American and British naval officials came up with a plan. It was called a convoy system. No longer would troop or supply ships cross the Atlantic alone. Instead, destroyers and other warships would surround them. All of these warships were equipped with radar. This allowed them to spot the hidden U-boats. The warships also carried torpedoes. And they had a new type of weapon. It was called a depth charge. Shaped like barrels, depth charges were filled with powerful explosives. Dropped over the sides of warships, they could destroy any U-boat beneath them.

Thanks to the convoy system, almost eight hundred U-boats were sunk. More than thirty thousand German sailors in these submarines were killed in the war. The Allies defeated the Germans in the long Battle of the Atlantic.

Were there spies working against the Nazis?

Yes. The use of spies in wartime is as old as war itself. And throughout World War II, thousands of American men and women served as spies. All kinds of people were spies—lawyers, movie stars, diplomats, sports figures, and teachers.

Serving as a spy was one of the war's most dangerous jobs. Being captured meant being shot. But it was also one of the war's most important jobs. Spies risked their lives to sneak into enemy-held territory. There the spies discovered where important factories and railroads were located so they could be bombed. They found out all they could about the size and strength of enemy troops. They discovered where the troops were headed.

To pass on the important information they gathered, spies used all kinds of special equipment. They carried tiny cameras hidden in jewelry and matchboxes. They also used radios disguised as suitcases. And they often hid maps and important messages in the heels of their boots.

Spies were not the only civilians who fought against the Germans. Thousands of men, women, and even children became resistance fighters. They hid themselves in countries the Germans had taken over. They attacked German supply lines. They also cut enemy telephone and telegraph lines. And they blew up railway lines and bridges. Like the spies, the brave resistance fighters were part of an important secret army.

The Enigma cipher machine was used by the Germans during WWII to write secret messages in code.

Fighting on Okinawa

Who gained control over the Pacific seas?

America's war against Japan was fought in the Pacific Ocean. Before WWII, battles at sea had always been fought by ships firing huge guns at each other. In the Pacific war, the United States and Japan fought each other with fighter planes. These planes were launched from the largest ships ever built. They were called aircraft carriers. They carried dozens of fighter planes.

The greatest naval battle of the Pacific war took place in June 1942. It was called the Battle of Midway. The Japanese sank one of America's largest carriers. But that was the only carrier the United States lost. American fighter planes destroyed four Japanese carriers. They were Japan's most important warships. From then on, the United States controlled the Pacific seas. There would be other large naval battles: one in the Philippine Sea and another in the Leyte Gulf. The Allies would win each one.

Where were the fiercest battles fought?

The fiercest battle of the entire war was the Battle of Stalingrad. In 1942, the German army invaded Russia. One of its main targets was the city of Stalingrad. The six-month battle that followed was the bloodiest in history. The combined deaths of soldiers and civilians on both sides numbered almost two million. In the end Germany was defeated.

The fiercest European battle that Americans fought in took place in the Ardennes Mountains in Belgium in December and January 1944. It was called the Battle of the Bulge. Some 81,000 American soldiers were either killed or wounded. But the Germans were defeated.

In the Pacific, terribly fierce battles took place on islands held by Japan. One of the worst of all was fought from April to June 1945 on the island of Okinawa. Before American troops were able to gain an important victory, the combined casualties of the Japanese and American forces totaled more than one hundred and fifty thousand.

How did the war change life in America?

Those who went off to war faced many hardships. But those they left behind at home had a hard time, too. American troops needed a lot of food. With so much food being sent to them, it was in short supply at home. The government rationed many foods. That meant people could only buy a small amount of certain items each month. Rationed items included sugar, milk, eggs, butter, and meat. To help the war effort, many families planted their own food in "Victory Gardens." Many schools also did their part. They set up Victory Gardens on school grounds or in public parks. Even city children who had never seen a farm joined in. They planted seeds, pulled weeds, and picked vegetables. Students were taught to "Dig for Victory."

No new cars were made during the war. People at home had to make their old cars last. Gasoline was strictly rationed. During 1942–1945, a family could only buy four gallons a week. That didn't take them very far. All the nation's rubber was used to make war products. There were no tires for sale. If a tire on the family car wore out, the family was out of luck. It was difficult, but most people did not complain. They wanted the soldiers fighting for them to have all they needed.

The war greatly changed the lives of women. A great many women had not worked outside the home. Now most men were away fighting. Women's help was badly needed. Hundreds of thousands of women went to work. Most took jobs in factories that made war weapons. They helped make airplanes, ships, and guns. Some became mechanics. They fixed damaged tanks and other vehicles. They did most of the jobs men had done. And they proved they could do them just as well.

Who were the Tuskegee Airmen?

More than a million African Americans contributed to the war effort during World War II. Among them was a special group of pilots, navigators, and ground crew. They were called the Tuskegee Airmen. Their job was to protect American bombers when they bombed enemy targets. Before the war ended, the Tuskegee Airmen flew more than one hundred missions. They destroyed or damaged more than 410 enemy airplanes. They wiped out 950 German gun placements on the ground. They even sank a battleship.

And they gained another great victory. Before the war, many white people believed that African Americans could not do difficult tasks. They even questioned African Americans' courage. The Tuskegee Airmen proved that they were very wrong.

The pilots pictured here are Tuskegee Airmen, a special unit of African Americans who fought in World War II.

How did the Allies trick the Germans on D-Day?

In spring, 1944, the Allies put together the largest invasion force in history. They were ready to cross the English Channel and enter German-occupied France. From there, they would be able to fight their way into Germany.

The Germans knew an invasion was coming. But where? The Allies knew it was terribly important that the spot be kept secret. Most German generals were sure that the invasion would take place at Pas-de-Calais. That was the closest French town to England. Plus, German planes had spotted huge numbers of planes, large guns, and military vehicles on the English coast. They were positioned directly across from Pas-de-Calais. The Germans moved troops and equipment into Pas-de-Calais.

But it was a trick. The Allied war equipment that the Germans spotted was not real. British movie studios had made it out of wood, cardboard, cloth, and rubber.

The trick worked. On June 6, 1944, in what was called D-Day, the Allies invaded. But they invaded in Normandy, France. It was much farther south than Pas-de-Calais. Though the Germans were surprised, many Allied soldiers were killed in the invasion. But the trick helped, and the Allies won the battle. By July 1944, the Allies were fighting their way across France and closing in on Hitler in Germany.

American troops invade Normandy beach in France on D-Day, June 6, 1944.

Anne Frank writing in her diary.

Why was Anne Frank hiding?

Anne Frank was a Jewish girl who lived with her family in the Netherlands. When the Germans invaded her country, they rounded up all the Jewish people. Then they sent them to horrible prisons called concentration camps. In order to avoid this, Anne and her family went into hiding when Anne was thirteen years old. For two years, they hid in secret rooms in her father's office building. Then someone reported them. Anne and her family were sent to a concentration camp. Anne, her mother, and her sister died. Only Anne's father survived.

During the two years she was in hiding, Anne kept a diary. In it she recorded her hopes, fears, and her thoughts on the war. Her father found and published his daughter's diary. For many, the diary was a glimpse into what it was like to be Jewish during the war. Readers were touched and inspired by Anne's courage.

Adolf Hitler and his Nazi party did many horrible things. None was worse than their plan to murder all Jewish people. The Nazis rounded up millions of European Jews and placed them in concentration camps throughout Europe. There were about twenty main concentration camps, but there were also more than 1,400 smaller camps. Approximately six million Jews plus other minority groups were killed. This slaughter of so many innocent people during WWII is called the Holocaust. We must remember these victims and their suffering so that a tragedy like this can never happen again.

Jews were forced to wear a yellow star with the German word for Jew, "Jude," to identify themselves. Wearing the star made Jews a target for mistreatment before and during WWII.

What ended the deadliest conflict in human history?

By the end of 1944, American, Russian, and British troops were fighting their way toward Berlin. In April 1945, they reached the German capital. Rather than be captured, Adolf Hitler committed suicide. On May 7, 1945, Germany surrendered. The war in Europe was finally over.

But the war in the Pacific against Japan went on. By the end of May 1945, American forces prepared to invade the island nation of Japan. American scientists had developed the most powerful weapon the world had ever known. It was an atomic bomb. Just one of these bombs could completely destroy an entire city.

By this time, American president Franklin Roosevelt had died. The new president was Harry S. Truman. He had an enormous decision to make. If he ordered an atomic bomb to be dropped on a Japanese city, thousands of civilians would be killed. But if that bomb were dropped, an invasion of Japan would probably be unnecessary and thousands of American soldiers would be spared.

In the end, President Truman decided to use the weapon. On August 6, 1945, an atomic bomb completely destroyed the city of Hiroshima. Still, the Japanese government refused to give in. Three days later, the city of Nagasaki was bombed. Now, the Japanese knew they had to surrender and did so on August 15. World War II was over at last.

All wars are terrible events. And World War II was the deadliest of them all. But some good things did come out of the conflict. Great inventions were created, including jet aircraft, helicopters, radar, and frozen foods. Great medical advances were also made. New medicines, such as penicillin, helped save lives. World War II also led to the creation of the United Nations. Its great task is to help nations solve their differences without going to war. The best outcome of World War II, however, was that the enemies of freedom were defeated.

WORLD WAR II TIMELINE

1931 SEPTEMBER 18 — Japan invades Manchuria.

1933 JANUARY 30 — Adolf Hitler becomes chancellor of Germany.

1937 JULY 7 — Japan invades China.

1939
MARCH 16 — Germany takes over Czechoslovakia.
SEPTEMBER 1 — Germany invades Poland. World War II begins.

1940
APRIL 9 — Germany invades Denmark and Norway.
MAY 10 — Germany invades France, Belgium, Luxembourg, and the Netherlands.
JUNE 22 — France surrenders to Germany.
JULY 1 — Nazi U-boats begin to sink Allies' ships in the Atlantic.
AUGUST 13 — Germany begins bombing British factories.
AUGUST 23-24 — Germans stage first bombing raids on London.

1941
JUNE 22 — German troops invade Russia.
DECEMBER 7 — Japan attacks Pearl Harbor.
DECEMBER 8 — The United States declares war on Japan.
DECEMBER 11 — Germany and Italy declare war on the United States.

1942
JUNE 4 — The Battle of Midway begins.
SEPTEMBER 13 — The Battle of Stalingrad begins.

1944
JUNE 6 — D-day—The Allies invade Normandy.
DECEMBER 16 — The Battle of the Bulge begins.

1945
APRIL 1 — The Battle of Okinawa begins.
APRIL 12 — President Roosevelt dies. Harry Truman becomes president.
APRIL 30 — Adolf Hitler commits suicide.
MAY 7 — Germany surrenders, ending the war in Europe.
AUGUST 6 — The Japanese city of Hiroshima is destroyed by an atomic bomb.
AUGUST 14 — Japan surrenders, ending World War II.
OCTOBER 24 — The United Nations officially begins.

For bibliography and further reading visit: http://www.sterlingpublishing.com/kids/good-question